Impossible is Stupid, what a title for a truly inspirational piece. Reading through the draft copy of the book, amidst my busy schedule was a time well invested. The book is filled with nuggets of wisdom to fight loneliness and live a fabulous life.

Impossible is Stupid, is a paradigm shift from conventional book writing. Osayi, I salute your courage in daring to write this book.

<u>Caution</u>: Read only when you are ready to make real decisions about your life.

– Segun Akiode, Nuggets for Nobles
http://segunakiode.wordpress.com

I loved it all.

– Jackie Paulson

My favorite chapter is 22 (stop cussin' yourself) This chapter really makes me cringe because I curse a lot when I'm angry and I never thought about how the words we use affect us more than the person we are using them on. It really makes me think twice about just shutting my mouth & not saying a word when I'm angry because if that's what it will take to make me better then amen to me!!

– Velia Ronquillo-Auk, Colorfulsweets, Stockton, CA

Funny, down to earth, practical and illuminating, the book will not only get you thinking but also acting. Although written primarily for women, any man reading it will obtain many useful hints on enhancing their relationship with the woman in their life.

- Ayo Adebamowo, UK, Author of A Life of Impact

www.ayodebamowo.blogspot.com

This book is a must read for every woman! **Impossible is stupid** when you make the seemingly impossible issues in life possible!

- Itohan Osayi, M, Wife and Mother, Lagos, Nigeria

Impossible is Stupid has been an added blessing in my life. I wish there was an android application and screensaver. What I like most is that each "beatitude" works without reading the paragraph that follows it, though you do want to read that. Thanks for your work.

– Dege Vernet, San Diego, CA

Impossible is Stupid is honest, straight-forward, and easy to read for folks like me that don't read much. I could see myself gifting a book like this to a few people I know.

– Mia Jones, Cre3sol, Baltimore MD

We Often Pray for God's Gift, but God's gift has been manifested to us through the life of this great daughter of Zion, Osayi Emokpae!! She is an inspiration to our generation today. Her book (**Impossible is Stupid**) will inspire, challenge, motivate and catapult you to another level. It will help you see your true self in the mirror, and challenge you to begin to take the necessary steps in God's direction as you unveil your true worth, and discover your true purpose; not just as a woman who has been through ups and downs in relationships, but as a child of God.

Woman thou art loosed, for truly **Impossible is Stupid**. A dynamic book! One of a Kind!! A must Read!!!

– Abies Adeyeri, Miami, FL

I love the down-to-earthness of **Impossible is Stupid** and how it doesn't lose the benefit of being a smooth easy read.

– Toyin Ajayi –Fadeyibi, Philadelphia, PA
http://toyeen4loveandmusic.blogspot.com

Impossible is Stupid is an encouraging book that gives you a chance to truly stop & reflect on your life (mentally, spiritually, emotionally). It's a smooth read that presents biblical truths in a natural and simple way that anyone can understand. It is not preachy but encourages the reader to engage the truths being presented in the book. It brings up real issues.

– Carla Jones, HTCF, Philadelphia, PA

Impossible is Stupid is fresh, inspiring, humorous, real...even men need to read the book.

— Chibuike Chuk Ejim, Click-On Internet Solutions, www.clickoninternet.com

Impossible is Stupid has many positive, inspirational, and motivational strategies to help women live up to their potential.

I am woman. Hear me roar!

— Chelsea Lee, Life of an Unofficial Pastor

Impossible is Stupid is a must read for everyone. It will help the married to forget whatever regrets they may have been carrying. Singles will have real hope not "guess-hope" from people who are not in their shoes. Pastors will have more realistic books to recommend for singles and parents.

It is great that such a book is written by a single lady. If it has been written by a married lady, it would have seemed as if the lady is writing only after she "escaped" singleness.

— Imose Osar-Emokpae, London, UK

Ever read something that made you smile from the inside, made you laugh out loud but all the while challenged you? **Impossible is Stupid** is a book of well placed words that will remind you to simply LIVE and to have a little fun while doing so!

— Cynthia Hampton, Philadelphia, PA

Impossible is Stupid

57 truths to help you beat loneliness and depression and live the fabulous life you always wanted.

Osayi Osar-Emokpae

Osayi Osar-Emokpae

Impossible is Stupid.

Impossible.Iyasostuff.com

ISBN-10: 1466420383
ISBN-13: 978-1466420380

DEDICATION

To my heavenly father, for encouraging me to do the
impossible every day.
To my earthly father, for inspiring me to be better than him,
and for selling the family car so I could have an education.
To my mother, for passing down her beauty, and still being
willing to wash my full head of hair whenever I ask.
To my older brother, for encouraging my crazy ideas, and
confirming that being me was better than being "normal."
To my younger brothers for reminding me that "stupid" is an
offensive word.

CONTENTS

ACKNOWLEDGMENTS   I

INTRODUCTION   3

THE END   5

57 CRUSH YOUR BIOLOGICAL CLOCK   7

56 EMBRACE BOREDOM   10

55 CREATE SOMETHING   12

54 STOP PRAYING ABOUT IT   14

53 FIND WORK YOU LOVE   16

52 IMAGINE DEATH   18

51 FIND YOUR PURPOSE   20

50 LET PAST MISTAKES GO   22

49 STOP BLAMING GOD   24

48 STOP HAVING SEX   26

47 LET GO OF SEXUAL ABUSE   29

46 EMBRACE THE LONGING   31

45 FOCUS ON TODAY   33

44 SMILE   35

43 READ   37

42 DON'T GET MARRIED!   39

41 FOCUS ON GOOD THINGS   41

40 MAINTAIN HEALTHY BOUNDARIES   43

39 OBSERVE NATURE   45

38 KEEP YOUR WORD   47

37 LAUGH   49

36 START A BUSINESS   51

35 END BAD HABITS   53

34 SPEAK   55

33 PAY OFF YOUR DEBT   57

32 THEIR THOUGHTS ARE NOT YOURS   59

31 SPEND TIME WITH KIDS   62

30 PICK INTIMATE FRIENDS WISELY   64

29 SET GOALS   66

28 GIVE   68

27 LEARN TO QUIT   71

26 ALWAYS DO THE RIGHT THING   73

25 LOSE SOME   75

24 CONSIDER THE LESS PRIVILEGED   77

23 GARBAGE IN, GARBAGE OUT   79

22 STOP CUSSIN' YOURSELF   81

21 IT'S SOMEONE ELSE'S PROBLEM   84

20 STOP WAITING ON GOD   86

19 SPEND TIME GETTING REFRESHED   88

18 IMAGINE SUCCESS   90

17 RECONNECT WITH OLD FRIENDS   92

16 MAKE NEW FRIENDS   94

15 MAKE TIME FOR PEOPLE   96

14 LEARN TO "LIGHT UP"   98

13 PLEASE REMEMBER MY NAME   100

12 BE PATIENT WITH LIFE   102

11 EMBRACE IMPERFECTION   105

10 YOU NEVER STOP THINKING   107

9 YOUR FUTURE IS SO BRIGHT   110

8 FREELY MAKE MISTAKES   113

7 MAKE PEOPLE FEEL NEEDED   115

6 OPINIONS ARE LIKE NOSES   117

5 GOD DOES NOT ORDAIN LONELINESS   119

4 DON'T YOU MISS ME?   121

3 THE FEMINIST LIE   123

2 GET MORE STUFF   125

1 KICK! BITE! SCREAM! FIGHT: 127

BULLY THE BULLIES!   127

0* (BONUS) FOCUS ON GOD'S LOVE   130

~~THE END~~   133

ACKNOWLEDGMENTS

Special thanks to those who read the first draft of this book on my blog iyasostuff.com. Your contributions and encouragement have been invaluable.
Special thanks to those who painstakingly edited and provided feedback – God is smiling upon you.

INTRODUCTION

Many years ago, I met the guy I planned to spend the rest of my life with. Everything was perfect – except that we argued all the time, we had absolutely nothing in common, we had different future aspirations and we were always putting ourselves in guilt-inducing compromising situations. One day in church, my pastor at the time (Pastor Stevens; Harvest Time Christian Fellowship, Philadelphia, PA) taught a sermon using **Galatians 5:1a** (NIV)

"It is for freedom that Christ has set us free."

I kept thinking to myself, "if Christ has set me free, then why don't I feel free? Why is this relationship so hard? Why does it feel like freedom is impossible? Why does it feel like this relationship is impossible?" And so began my long and painful journey to finding this freedom that Christ died to give me; this fabulous life where **impossible is stupid**.

The story ended well for him and me.
We both ended up living happily ever after…separately.

I later realized that I had made many relationship decisions out of loneliness and fear of being alone, and the consequences were painful. I wrote this book to remind myself never to go there again, never to be that person again.

So where it feels like I'm yelling at you, please don't take it personally – unless you should. Where it seems like common sense, please bear with me, it just means you're much wiser than I am. Where it seems tongue in cheek…well what can I say, I'm multifaceted…

If something resonates with you take it, and the rest, you're free to take with a grain of salt. And oh, don't forget to grab your free action guide at: **impossible.iyasostuff.com**

Let's begin…at the end…

~~The Beginning~~

The End.

"Behold, I am the **LORD**, the God of all flesh: is there **anything too hard** for me?" **~ God**

(Jeremiah 32:27; KJV)

So what do you think?
Is there anything too hard for God?

57 CRUSH YOUR BIOLOGICAL CLOCK

"Crush your biological clock!" – Ms. Sherry Holmes (Full Gospel Word and Worship Center; Columbia, SC)

"If you don't get married by 21 or you are not at least dating the man you are to marry by 20 then you will die a miserable wretch!" This is what the voice in our heads tell us over and over again. Constantly tormenting us with thoughts that life will never happen the way we want it to, and that life will never be the happy place we always dreamt it would be.

Then society comes and tells us that if we don't have our children by 30 not only will we be too tired to take care of them, but if we are lucky enough to have any children, they will all be born with a new rare form of down's syndrome, and we would wish that we never even thought of having children.

So we try to fight the voices of society, the voices of the well meaning family and friends urging us to settle down because "our clocks are ticking" and so we do stupid things to try to fix this "singleness" problem before it's too late, before we end up with our worst nightmare. We try to fight the voices in our heads, we try to tell them to be quiet, we try to remind the voices of that one lady we watched on the news a few years ago, or we heard from our friends a few years ago, we can't quite remember her name, or their names, but we know that one day not that long ago we heard of that lady who had a child at like 50 or 70 (or whatever we consider old) and the child was born healthy. We try to comfort ourselves with these thoughts, but the voices inside our head get louder and louder as the days go by and Mr. Right has gotten stuck in the rat race of life or has gotten lost and refuses to ask for directions to meet us, his very own Mrs. Right, and as the voices get louder we begin to lose hope, we begin to feel that the voices are right, society is right, our friends and family are right.

We forget that the same people urging us to get married are miserable in their marriages, we forget that this was the same society that told us we would never get over our asthma, and yet here we were breathing freely without any assistance, we forget that this was the same voice that told us we would never pass Human Anatomy and Physiology because we did not have enough money to buy the textbook, and the words seemed like a foreign language to us, we forget all the things that they had predicted actually rarely happened. We buy the fear from them, in exchange for our hope, our lives, and then we watch them as they skip off to find the next victim to rob of all their joy, then we sigh and get angry and depressed because they stole our peace from us, but it wasn't their fault, we let them.

We let them wave the stupid paper clocks in our faces. We let them determine the meaning for our lives, we let them use their words to destroy us, we let them run over us with their stupid lies, that even they had begun to believe...

But we don't have to let them anymore, we don't have to believe the lies anymore, we don't have to exchange our priceless hope for their stupid paper clocks. God did not give us a spirit of fear...now is the time. Let us crush these so-called biological clocks that give us nothing but fear, and encourage us to make stupid decisions. Let us crush these biological clocks that hurt us and rob us of the fabulous lives that Jesus died to give us. These clocks that not only hurt us, but hurt many generations after us.

It is time. We need you.

56 EMBRACE BOREDOM

"The beauty of doing nothing is that it teaches you to clear your mind and relax." – Richard Carlson, PH.D. (Don't Sweat the Small Stuff…and it's all Small Stuff)

When was the last time you took time to be bored? Just to give yourself time to breathe and think and reflect on life so far. We find ourselves making the same mistakes over and over again because we don't give ourselves time to be bored and to reflect. We date the same joker over and over again, only each time he comes back with a different name or a different smile or a different complexion, but each time he comes back saying the same things and getting the same responses from us. We fall for the same lies, the same sweet nothings, the same things we said we would never do again, but there we are falling for it.

We hate being bored, we hate having nothing to do, we hate feeling like we're not being entertained, but life was never meant to be about entertainment. Do I look like a clown, does this look like a circus? If you're looking for entertainment go to the circus, if you're looking to live a fulfilled life, don't let boredom stop you, instead embrace it, cherish it, use it to brainstorm on that great idea you always wanted. Use it to think about all the mistakes you made in life and how you plan on avoiding those mistakes again. Use it to write that book you always meant to write but just "never had the time."

It's time, we're waiting for you. We're tired of your excuses, your complaining, your everything else. We need you now more than we have ever needed you before, so it's time for you to use your boredom wisely. Yes there will be time for you to have fun, and life is indeed meant to be fun, but if you fill every waking moment with something to amuse you, then you will never accomplish anything worthwhile – which makes me concerned for you, because after all, if you were not meant for something worthwhile, then why exactly are you here?

55 CREATE SOMETHING

"…Don't wait for permission, or worry about doing something different, or invent reasons why you don't have authority. Somebody has to make the first move. It might as well be you. Change your world, today." – Seth Godin

Perhaps no one ever told you before, well I'm going to tell you now. No one can make you feel less lonely, but you. When you realize this, when this sinks in and you start believing it, things will change dramatically. You are the only one that can get advice, that can seek help, that can seek encouragement, that can become the person you want to be.

There is so much within you that we need in this life. If you don't create those things that you were meant to create, then no one else will – not like you. They may create similar things, because after all we all must survive, with or without you, but we would be so much better with you. We need you to create those dreams that you always had. We need you to decide to be that person you always wanted to be.

We need you to create, to innovate, to do the unique and creative things that only you know how to do. And the best part about it is that when you are in your zone – creating things that are uniquely you – you will be too busy doing amazing things to be lonely.

There is no more "tomorrow," there are no more excuses.

You can no longer say that you are not smart enough, or educated enough, or rich enough, or anything else enough. The fact that you are you, means that you are enough and LADY We need you to create something uniquely and spectacularly you!

Go ahead! We're waiting.

54 STOP PRAYING ABOUT IT

"Prayer is not to inform 'poor, misinformed God' about how bad your situation is! Because most people are ignorant of this, problems, need, and urgency occupy a large percentage of prayer! If telling God about problems and how bad they are were removed from people's prayers, not much would be left. That's why I advise most women to quit praying for their husbands." – Andrew Wommack (A Better Way to Pray)

Yes! We're tired of your prayers. We're tired of your "hoping" and "thinking" about it all. You feel lonely when you wake up, you feel lonely when you go to sleep, everything you talk about focuses on how lonely you are. When you are by yourself you talk to yourself about your loneliness, when you are with people you talk about how being in the crowd makes you feel lonely, and then you have the audacity to cry to God to take away the loneliness.

Hello! Haven't you realized by now that the problem is not God. He is not sitting on his throne waiting for you to cry loud enough to solve your problems. He is not hoping that you finally find the keys to speaking to him, so that he can finally answer your prayer…God is not like that.

He has already answered your prayers when he told you that the fruit of your new spirit is love, joy, peace etc. (Galatians 5:22-23). Did God create you to be miserable? Is God trying to teach you something by making you lonely? Of course not.

So stop praying about it! It's time you figured it out that all these years of praying have not changed anything. Either God is refusing to answer your prayers or he already has (and you haven't realized it), and trust me it's not the former.

53 FIND WORK YOU LOVE

"Have the courage to follow your heart and intuition. They somehow already know what you truly want to become." – Steve Jobs

Your alarm clock goes off and you're miserable. It's time to go to work and you're miserable. The only thing you like about your job is lunch time, which is only supposed to be thirty minutes long, but you always manage to extend it to an hour.

Of course you spend the entire time during your blissful lunch break singing the songs of regret with your other coworkers about how much you hate "Mr. Bossman" and how you could have been an artist or a writer or something else, but instead you are stuck here.

Well no one told you to stay there. Yes you may have bills, and yes you may have kids that are relying on you and, yes you may have all the other things that make you feel like you are stuck, but you know what, being stuck is only in your mind. You make your own decisions.

Remember those days when you would do things and the time flew by so quickly. Remember the times you felt as if you were in sync with your work, whether you were writing, or drawing, or painting or whatever else it was, but you were in your zone, you were doing something that made you smile and gave you energy.

Guess what? I have a secret to share with you – you can go back to that time. Not literally of course, we definitely don't have a "go-back-in-time-machine." But you can actually find work doing something that you enjoy doing. You can actually make that thing that you thought would always be a hobby, into something that can actually sustain you.

Were you voted most talkative in school, guess what? You can be a motivational speaker, were you voted Ms. Popular? Guess what? You can go into sales or public relations, it's time to stop wasting your skills and start using them. If you don't who will?

52 IMAGINE DEATH

"Take a moment and write your final chapter, the way you want it to be. And as you do, think about your life from this point forward. Forget the past, because you can't change it." – Craig Groeschel

So you're dead, you're lying in the grave and your friends and family come up to talk about you.

"well she went to work every day...and umm she didn't complain about it some days."

Is this the legacy you want to leave behind? Steve Jobs died, and the whole world mourned. My ex-coworker died and most people didn't even remember his name. Why? One had chosen to live life to the fullest and excelled at it, the other was merely existing.

The thing about this life is that it is extremely short. One minute you are on the playground learning how to move your legs to propel the swing, and the next minute you're old and in your dying bed, what happened in between? Did your life matter? Did your life make a difference? Were you too busy working at that miserable place that you actually forgot to live? Were you too busy waiting and looking for Mr. Right that you actually forgot to enjoy the life that God gave you? Were you too busy telling everyone about how miserable your life was that you forgot to share in other people's joys and celebrations? Were you so busy being jealous every time somebody announced their engagement or the birth of their child that most people avoided even telling you about their good news?

What if I told you I knew the exact date and time you would die, and that you didn't have much time left? What would you do differently?

When you leave this earth, how will you be remembered, what will people say about you at your funeral? It may not matter to you then, because after all you'll be dead. But it matters now. Because now you have the opportunity to change your story.

Imagine you were living this life for the second time, and you now know that you can't fail, what would you do differently?

51 FIND YOUR PURPOSE

"…[M]an is created on earth for a three-fold purpose like God. Except we discover this purpose, life is a waste whether one is an ordained minister or not, whether a Christian or a non-Christian." Dr. Osaren Philips Emokpae (From Minimum to Maximum: Twelve Keys to Succeed in the Contemporary World)

My computer has a purpose, my car has a purpose, even my dishes have a purpose. What's yours?

You are here for a reason, what is that reason? Don't tell me you don't know, and you have no way of knowing…

What is it that **gets you excited**? What is it that if you never got paid for it, you would still keep doing it? What is it that if you could never do it again you would be devastated? For me it's writing. For my friend it's teaching. What's yours?

You are **here for a reason** – find that reason, harness that power and start living the fabulous life you were meant to!

For we are God's workmanship, created in Christ Jesus to do good works, which God prepared in advance for us to do.
— EPHESIANS 2:10 NIV

50 LET PAST MISTAKES GO

"In the shadow of my hurt, forgiveness feel like a decision to reward my enemy. But in the shadow of the cross, forgiveness is merely a gift from one undeserving soul to another." – Andy Stanley (It Came from Within!: The Shocking Truth of What Lurks in the Heart)

Yes you shouldn't have kissed that guy or slept with the other guy, or gone to that party, or gone to that guy's house, but guess what? You did and guess what? You shouldn't have and guess what else ? It's time for you to forgive yourself and let it go. The voices in your head will tell you constantly what a fool you are to make such a mistake, and how no one would accept you if they knew of the time you made out with your best friend's ex or masturbated or were addicted to pornography or messed around with a girl, or any of the other taboos in society. But guess what? The world will go on. We are all carrying our own secrets within us. The same thing that you think is too hideous to share, is the same thing that the girl beside you on the train is carrying around with her – too ashamed to share as well.

We all have past mistakes. Things we could have done better, people we could have treated better, choices we could have made but didn't. It's time to let it go, and live in the moment.

You can't change the past, only the present. Forgive yourself, and anyone else that disappointed you in the past. Don't torment yourself thinking whether life would have been better if you had done things differently. Don't keep rehashing the arguments and wondering if you'd have been married by now if you hadn't been so stupid….let it go. Don't think it's impossible to live a happy life now. Don't think that God will never forgive you or give you another opportunity since you messed up the 365 opportunities he had already given you. Just let it go, forgive yourself, move on, the rest of the world already has.

49 STOP BLAMING GOD

"In times of crisis it's easy to shift responsibility – and blame – on God…At some point we become God's hands and feet – without us His work does not get done. And His work is not just preaching, praying or proselytizing. It's mowing yards, making violins, building houses, delivering pizza, or teaching school kids – with excellence." – Dan Miller (Don't I Just Wait on God)

You didn't get what you always wanted, it must be God's will. The guy you were in love with since kindergarten marries that girl you never liked, it must have been God's will. You get fired from your job, God must have been trying to teach you something. You get deathly ill with no cure in sight, obviously God was trying to get your attention.

If God were my earthly father and you accused him of the things you accused God of doing, I would take off my wig and pummel you to the ground. How can a loving, kind, gracious, gentle father like mine send you diseases just to get your attention? Or purposely hurt your heart by "letting" the guy you really liked (the one everyone, especially you, thought you would marry) marry someone else? If God hadn't given you the control of your life, then yes maybe you could blame God for your bad decisions. And if God hadn't given other people the control of their lives, then yes you could blame God for the evil they did. But God has given you the control of your life and he has provided you with everything you need, if you choose to use it.

God is a good God. If you truly believed that premise then you would understand that it would be impossible for him to do things purposely just to hurt you. Everything God does is good and he said he will not withhold any good thing from you, and he also said that he who finds a wife finds a good thing… **God only wants good things for you**.

No he does not control whether you get married or not. And no he does not control whether you get to work on time or not, which determines whether or not you will be fired. And no he does not control whether you accomplish his purpose for you or not…He has given you (and everyone else for that matter) the free will to make decisions. He can guide you, if you ask for his guidance, but he will not force you or anyone else to do anything. He loves you and wants the best for you. Whenever you're feeling sad and thinking that the reason you are single is because God wants you to be single. Stop yourself – if God wanted you to be single, you wouldn't have the desire to be married.

48 STOP HAVING SEX

"Without the union of marriage, the union of bodies is a parody and mockery of itself. Bereft of its proper point and context, sexual intimacy outside of marriage does not bring us into the lover's embrace, but merely exposes us to the stranger's stare, and reduces us to the means of someone else's pleasure." – Michael Lawrence (Sex is Not About Waiting)

Sex is great! It's natural, and human beings were created to enjoy sex. The problem is not that sex is a bad thing or that sex cannot feel great, the problem is that we have esteemed sex to the level of a god. We think that if we are not "sexually compatible" with someone then we should not marry them. Seriously, what does that even mean? It means that someone doesn't know how to satisfy us sexually? And that disqualifies him because? Well if that is the case then there is no point in any of us trying to walk or talk or feed ourselves or dress ourselves since it took us years to learn some of these things. The physical act of sex can be learned and even the most obtuse man out there can learn how to please a woman, and many obtuse men have learned.

The challenge is not just pleasing a woman in bed, but being a man outside of the bedroom. A man of godly character, the kind of man that is so committed to something, that not even the most enticing thing can distract him. The man that has learned self control. The man that has learned to cherish a woman beyond the physical pleasure that she can provide him, the man that has learned that true intimacy and true fulfillment is more than just being able to show you a "good time."

Yes sex can feel great, can relieve stress, can do all sorts of wonderful things, but if you're expecting sex to keep the relationship, you are in for a very startling surprise. There will always be someone who is better looking than you. There will always be someone who is "more sexually compatible" with him than you.

The beauty of sex is that it binds two people as one. When sex is outside of marriage, there is a false sense of security that is immediately shattered whenever any little thing arises. You may say that it doesn't mean much since everyone is doing it, and that if you love somebody and want to spend the rest of your life with him, then why isn't it okay? You may say that it's a personal decision that doesn't affect anyone else, so why should it matter whether or not you're sleeping with him. Well it does matter, because it matters to God. Sex is natural, but premarital sex is like trying to breath underwater, it's unnatural, and it always hurts.

But hey it's a free world, do whatever makes you happy, and when you come crying to me about heartache, I won't even say "I told you so."

If you do what is right, will you not be accepted? But if you do not do what is right, sin is crouching at your door; it desires to have you, but you must master it. — GENESIS 4:7 NIV

47 LET GO OF SEXUAL ABUSE

"Whoever fights monsters should see to it that in the process he does not become a monster. And if you gaze long enough into an abyss, the abyss will gaze back into you." – Friedrich Nietzsche

Sexual abuse is a monster, straight from the pits of hell. Anyone who has been abused, which I believe is more people than are willing to admit it, can still remember the moment as if it was yesterday, because in their minds it will always be yesterday. The thing about monsters is that all they have is their bark, because their puny little teeth fall off whenever they try to bite. We are scared of what people will think of us if they were to ever find out. We are scared of the anger we feel toward the people that abused us and the others that knew about it and said nothing.

We are angry and confused and feel like we can never accomplish much. We feel like we are worthless, since we were treated like we were. But we are not worthless, we are priceless, amazingly beautiful creatures, and sadly those people were too blind (or stupid) to see it.

So we're not going to try to hide it and forget it any more, we are not going to try to pretend like it didn't happen while having nightmares about it every night. Instead we are going to look the monster in the face one last time, and tell it goodbye. Repeat it after me. Goodbye. Now say it like you mean it. GOODBYE! Because from now on that monster is no longer going to be ours.

If you have to find someone to talk to, then find them and talk to them, even if you have to pay a professional. If you have to confront the person, go ahead, confront them and let them know they no longer have the power to rent space in your mind. The main thing is letting it go quickly before we become the monster we hate, because the other thing about monsters is that they are as contagious as the plague.

46 EMBRACE THE LONGING

"Our bodies need constant nourishment, right? Hunger is simply a trigger designed by God to stimulate a necessary response…The satisfying response to physical hunger is food and drink. The satisfying response to emotional hunger is love (among other things). The satisfying response to mental hunger is knowledge. And the only satisfying response to spiritual hunger is God." – Gwen Smith (Satisfy Your Hunger)

Yes you find him attractive, and yes your senses tingle every time you're around him. So what? What is so wrong with being attracted to an attractive man. God MADE WOMEN to be attracted to men, it's natural.

As women, we often think that we shouldn't have those longings or that attraction. We feel as if when that guy kissed us and we actually kissed him back it meant we had lost our salvation, and were hopelessly destined for hell. No! That is not true. Maybe you shouldn't have been in the situation where the guy could try to kiss you or grope at you in the dark (especially since you were on your period, and you know how extra-sensitive you are when you are on your period), and maybe you should never have even agreed to spending time with this guy who called himself "a Christian" but really didn't know much about God and you knew it. Maybe you shouldn't have been so desperate to have someone to talk to or talk about when other people talked about being in relationships that you ended up with sir-kissy-face...but regardless, it happened, he kissed you, you were attracted to him, congratulations, you're human.

Now let the Joseph spirit move you and flee from that man as quickly as you can. There is nothing wrong with you being attracted to a man, but don't put yourself in a situation where things can happen that you would rather they didn't.

Embrace the fabulous God-given desire, cherish and protect it for that right man and that right time.

You think embracing the longing while waiting for the right man is impossible? Well obviously you didn't get the memo.

45 FOCUS ON TODAY

"Every day, we lose another 1,440 minutes that will never return. Farewell, minutes! Goodbye, opportunities…This is a friendly reminder to stop living mindlessly. Spend your days in pursuit of joy and adventure. Help someone and create something that will endure. The end is (always) near." – Chris Guillebeau

For some reason yesterday seems so much more pleasant and so much more exotic after it has passed. In contrast today seems hopeless and miserable because after all, it's not as amazing as "yesterday" was. It's almost as if the older we get the more fabulous the past was.

We spend so much time longing for what was, and what could be. We spend so much time regretting and hoping…We forget to live and enjoy today. Life was not meant to go downhill after birth, it was meant to get better and better. As we learned the truth that the world does not revolve around us we were also supposed to learn that God is always on our side. We were supposed to learn to love the journey of life. We were supposed to learn to appreciate the beauty of life. We were supposed to learn to be thankful that God would give us the privilege of living this fabulous life that he created especially for us. But what do we do instead? We complain and waste time.

How about we try something different. Instead of worrying about what could happen, or what you would like to happen that may never happen, focus on today. Stop focusing on the fears and the worries of the past. Stop making decisions based on the past and the worries of the future. Focus on the beauty of today.

Today life is beautiful. I have food to eat, I have clothes to wear, I am healthy, and I am safe.

If nothing else, Today is good, so focus on Today.

44 SMILE

We all have the ability to control our emotions. We like to use excuses like "oh! I'm on my time of the month," or "oh I was just so angry!" or "oh, I can't help but feel depressed!" Please excuse my language, but all of that is just foolishness. If we couldn't control our emotions, then it would be silly for God to tell us to be patient with one another, or not to be moved by what we see.

I'm not a psychologist, and I don't play one on T.V, but what I do know is that the whole world changes when we smile. What we thought would devastate us may not seem so devastating anymore. People say frowning uses more muscles and it makes us get more wrinkled so we shouldn't frown. I say all that is hogwash. Smiling is hard, and some of the "smiliest" people are some of the most wrinkled people, but that should not be our focus.

Smiling makes us happier, makes us see everything better, helps us to go through hard things much more easily. Smiling helps us by reminding us that we've been through hard days like this one, but they never last. Smiling reminds our bodies of what it feels like to be happy, and subconsciously urges our minds to find that happy place again.

So do you want a fabulous life, or do you want a mediocre life? You get to choose. I hope you choose wisely.

43 READ

"We can only change our lives and create a world of our own if we first understand how such a world is constructed, how it works, and the rules of the game. And that means we have to study the world and how we are in it." – Michael E. Gerber (The E Myth Revisited)

When God asked King Solomon for one request, he said that he wanted to be wise. I never really understood that as a child. The older I get though, I am beginning to realize how amazingly simple yet amazingly brilliant this request was. Wisdom is the only thing that no one can take away from you. Today we have access to thousands of years of wisdom, and what do we do with this wisdom? Nothing. We are too busy watching T.V.

People often ask me how I have so much time to get things done, they think I must be a very productive person. The truth is that I waste way more time than I would even like to admit. But the beautiful thing is that I took Dave Ramsey's advice and "put a brick through my T.V."

There is so much knowledge out in the world. And there are so many wise people in the world. Sadly, the majority of people are unwise (and dare I say foolish). If the main way of getting access to some of the most brilliant minds in the world is through their books and I don't read them, then what does that make me?

If the wealthiest two percent of people in the world own more than half of the wealth in the world... and I'll repeat it again – If the wealthiest two percent (2%) of people in the whole entire world own more than fifty percent (50%) of all the wealth in the world, do you think they probably know something you don't?

If you're getting angry instead of learning from them, what does that say about you?

42 DON'T GET MARRIED!

"I learned that day that there is no more lonely state than being in a lonely marriage." – Julie Metz

I know, I know…you're probably thinking "What!!!! All I can ever think about is getting married! I'm so lonely!"

If marriage was the solution to loneliness, then more people would be satisfied in their marriages. The problem is that many people are waiting to meet this person that is supposed to "complete" them. It will be a sad day if you ever meet that person. Do you understand the amount of pressure you would be placing on another human being if you were expecting him to make you "feel complete." Yes it sounds romantic for someone to tell me that I "complete them." But seriously, I can barely complete my sentences, how am I supposed to complete a whole complex being? What if this guy you're hoping to marry was expecting you to make him feel whole? What if he was expecting you to make him happy, and never be depressed again for the rest of your lives together? You're barely learning how to be happy in your own life, how stressful would it be for you to get married and realize that he expects you to be the clown in his three-ring circus.

I completely understand your desire for marriage, and there is nothing wrong with that desire…The problem though is eliminating loneliness cannot be your sole purpose for getting married. No one can ever make you feel less lonely. And believe it or not, some of the loneliest people on the planet are married people.

The best thing you can do for you and your future spouse is to deal with your loneliness before you get married. Find comfort outside of people and things. Because there is nothing as miserable as a miserably lonely married person who thought their spouse would fix all their problems (just Google **married and lonely**)…

But if as you read this book, you're saying to yourself: "I'd rather be miserably married than be alone." Well young lady, take out your clown shoes and buckle your seatbelt – it's going to be a very bumpy one-woman circus.

41 FOCUS ON GOOD THINGS

"Good things happen to people who expect good things" – Zig Ziglar (See You at the Top)

Why is it that when good things happen we quickly forget, but when bad things happen we spend years trying to recover? The thing about life is that it's so easy to think about all the bad things that have happened to us in the last decade…even though there are so many more good things to think about. We remember the regrets, we remember the mistakes, but we often forget the good decisions, and the proud moments.

Life doesn't always make sense. If you have a bad day at work, you can't always trace it to something you did wrong that day, sometimes it has to do with you, and other times it doesn't. Instead of wasting time trying to figure out why you are angry or sad or depressed, think about a time you were happy, think about a time when good things happened, focus on that time, and try to create more of those kinds of experiences. If drinking tea makes you happy, spend more time drinking tea, if writing a blog makes you happy, spend more time writing a blog, but if you find out that you're not happy all of a sudden, go back to a time you were happy and focus on that time.

If something bad unexpectedly happens, take it in stride, think of five other positive things that happened and focus on those things instead.

If it was easy to focus on good things, I wouldn't have to write this book. It's not easy. It's not automatic. But it's worth it, and you're worth much more.

40 Maintain Healthy Boundaries

"No' is a complete sentence." Anne Lamott

The beautiful thing about being an adult is that you have the power to decide who your friends will be, and whether or not you want to do certain things. You can choose to help those around you, or not. There is no point feeling guilty about your decision to choose. That's what life is about - choices. Sometimes people will be hurt, and other times they will be appreciative. But if you get your sense of self or your self-esteem from people, you will always be in an emotional rollercoaster not quite knowing when you will be up, or when you will be down next.

It's easy to think that people will like you more if you do whatever they tell you to do, but it's quite the opposite. People don't appreciate pushovers – they use them. And people who are pushovers always feel horrible about themselves.

It's unfair to you and to your friends for you to give them so much power over your thoughts and your decisions. True friends deserve to know you and to love you for who you are.

If they never get to really know you because you are too afraid of hurting their feelings by telling them no, then what is the point? Your friendship is a sham, and your life is a bigger sham!

To have a healthy self-image, you have to be prepared to say NO sometimes. You have to learn to say NO, so that you can freely say YES to the things you really want to do. When you have healthy boundaries, people will respect you more, but more importantly, you will like yourself more.

What's the point of living a fabulous life if it's somebody else's idea of a fabulous life?

39 OBSERVE NATURE

"The earth has music for those who listen." –William Shakespeare

Sometimes we get so caught up in the chaos of our lives that we think the whole world is in chaos, but that's not true. The world is a beautifully organized place.

There is a state park close to my house, and I love going there and walking around, observing the beauty of nature. I could live in that park! (too bad we get kicked out of the park by sunset). The green is so lush and quiet and serene and calm and beautiful. The insects crawl around looking for food, while the birds chirp peacefully…and the water trickles quietly through the little water ways all around the park…

Nature doesn't just calm us, it also reminds us that if God can create something so beautiful, with so much detail, how much more will he take care of us?

"Much more" – I love that phrase. Every time the Bible compares God's love for us to something else, it always says it's "much more." It's almost as if God used the most beautiful word we have to help us understand his love for us, but even the most beautiful word was not enough to truly explain the depths of God's love for us.

We spend so much time worrying and thinking and hoping that God will come through, hoping that God will finally figure out what a mess our lives have become, when instead we can just focus and realize that before the beginning of time, God thought about us and planned a fabulous life for us.

Do you think God put all those intricate details in you for no reason? Girl please.

38 KEEP YOUR WORD

"To measure yourself on the character scale, does what you do match up with what you say? Are you the same person no matter whom you are with, do you make decisions that are best for others when another choice would benefit you? Are you quick to recognize others for their efforts and contributions to your success?" – Dr. Osaren Philips Emokpae (Guilty or not Guilty)

I once dated a guy who told me I was "finicky," which sadly I thought meant fickle. I was so upset that he thought my words couldn't be trusted that every relationship after that, I promised myself that I would never give another guy the opportunity to think I was "finicky." I later realized that "finicky" was quite different from fickle, but it was a little too late.

There are times that I have disappointed friends because I promised to do something but end up unable to do it, those have been some of the most hurtful times. I hate going back on my word. Sadly some people don't care about that. They don't care if they tell you that they will be some place or do something for you or anything else, they just do whatever works for them at the time. And of course it's never their fault.

There's no point in being friends with people who are fickle. While fickle people are usually very kind people, they are very unreliable, they will cause you more hurt than you can imagine, leave you stranded more times than you expect, and make you feel worthless since your time is not as valuable to them as theirs.

There are times when things happen and you can't help it. It happens, your friends will forgive you. But if you make a habit of it, then my suggestion is that your friends find other friends.

There is something about a person who keeps their word no matter how much of an inconvenience it is for them. When you break your word you inconvenience other people and you deplete the trust out of the relationships. When people don't trust you, they don't want to be around you, and they try to avoid inconveniencing themselves for you (since they never quite know if you will keep your word).

If I can't trust your word, I can't trust you.

37 LAUGH

"If we couldn't laugh we would all go insane." – *Robert Frost*

If life wasn't happening to us, we would spend so much time laughing at all the crazy things we experience. I remember one time when the folks at my job were trying to get a guy to move from one cubicle to another. They sent him an email, then a few other emails. Then a lady came in to ask him if he had gotten the email, then a guy came to ask him, then another lady brought the personal belongings of the person who would be taking over the cubicle and started placing the items on the desk, without saying anything to him. Then another guy came in to ask if he had gotten the email – all within a matter of minutes….The rest of us were amused as we wondered what was going on. By the time the guy finally got all his stuff and moved out of the cubicle he looked a little perplexed, while the rest of us just laughed and shook our heads…

Work would probably be more humorous if it wasn't so strange. Strange people doing strange things that you still can't quite understand. All you can do to keep yourself from being confused is to shrug, laugh and let it go.

Laughter is good medicine, it is God's gift to us to remind us that things could always be worse. Many people have realized how powerful laughter can be and have even started **laughter clubs**. Whether you join a club or not, the important thing is learning to laugh at situations, at yourself, at life, because after all "he who laughs last (and first), laughs best."

When was the last time you had a good belly-shaking-tear-jerking-snot-producing laugh? That long?

36 START A BUSINESS

"Actually, the best part of being an entrepreneur is not the control you gain over wealth, but the chance to handpick the people you surround yourself with and create an organizational culture that is completely in sync with who you are." – Jonathan Fields (Career Renegade)

What is it that you've always been passionate about? What is it that if you didn't have to worry about money you would do? What is it that gets you excited and invigorated, that if you had to do it every day for the rest of your life you would be delighted?

Whatever it is, think of ways that you can start working on it. Think of ways that you can serve people with it. Think of ways that you can meet needs with it. **You don't necessarily have to quit your day job right away, but think of ways to start a business doing what you enjoy doing.**

There's this guy, Cheeming Boey, who makes money from selling paper cups that he decorated with sharpies – he sells some of them for $400 each. So what exactly is your excuse? Even if you don't start the business right away, start working on a business plan, or start thinking of where your business will be located, who you would like to work with, what kinds of clients you would like to have. Start dreaming again about all the big and fabulous things you would like to do.

There is something that happens when your passion becomes your life's work...Trust me, you need to do this – for us, for you.

35 END BAD HABITS

"Good habits are hard to acquire but easy to live with. Bad habits are easy to acquire but hard to live with." – Zig Ziglar (See You at the Top)

Bad habits come in many different categories; bad habits that cost us money, bad habits that cost us relationships, bad habits that steal our time, bad habits that steal our youth, bad habits that fill us with regrets, bad habits that embarrass us and bring us shame…and the list goes on.

The thing about habits is that the only person that can stop a bad habit is me. It doesn't matter how much others try to force me or convince me or help me. The only person that can make the decision and make the change is me.

Think of all the things you could be doing with the money you spend on your addiction. Think of all the time you could be spending doing other more worthwhile things. Think of all the people that you can't talk to or look in the eye because you feel as if the smell of your bad habit follows you everywhere. Think of the fabulous life you're not living because of your stinkin' bad habit.

Then think of the person you would like to be, think of the person you would like your children to have as a parent, or the kind of friend you would like to be, or the kind of wife that you would like to be. Is the bad habit worth it?

Bad habits drain us of our self respect, and of things that matter most to us. **You know your bad habits. Pick one, and choose to end it**. Give yourself a month or so of replacing one bad habit with a good habit, and you will be surprised how refreshed you feel when you realize that you are no longer a slave of your bad habits – that is unless you are one of those people that actually enjoy slavery.

34 SPEAK

"In Germany, they first came for the Communists, and I didn't speak up because I wasn't a Communist. Then they came for the Jews, and I didn't speak up because I wasn't a Jew. Then they came for the trade unionists, and I didn't speak up because I wasn't a trade unionist. Then they came for the Catholics and I didn't speak up because I wasn't a Catholic. Then they came for me – and by that time there was nobody left to speak up." - Martin Niemoller

Injustice still exists. And we need people like you to speak for truth. We need people like you to speak – not to hurt other people's feelings, or to deprive them of their rights, but to protect those who can't speak for themselves. There are many things that I am passionate about, but I will never be as passionate as you are about those things you are passionate about.

Imagine what life would be like if Martin Luther King Jr. never spoke up for civil rights. Yes, I know you may be thinking, well I don't have something that important going on with me. But it doesn't really matter. Whatever it is, wherever it is, if injustice exists, it's up to you, it's up to me. If it's at work and people are gossiping about coworkers, if it's in church and people are purposely staying away from the weird looking girl. Wherever it is, if injustice exists it's up to you to speak.

Not only do we need you to speak, YOU need you to speak! If you don't speak then you will always be a shadow of yourself. You will always wonder what would have happened if you had spoken, you will always wonder how the world would have changed if only you had the courage to speak. Instead of wondering and hoping, SPEAK!

33 PAY OFF YOUR DEBT

"To preserve our independence, we must not let our rulers load us with perpetual debt. We must make our election between economy and liberty, or profusion and servitude." – Thomas Jefferson

There's a song that came out recently and one of my favorite lines in that song is "I just want it all." This line is so descriptive of most of us today. We don't want much, we just want it all, and we don't want to have to wait either.

What do we want? – Everything!
When do we want it? – Now!

The problem is that this lack of patience leads us to make horrible decisions. Then we are tied down to things that we buy, and have to stay at miserable jobs because we need the money to pay our bills. Credit can be useful, but most times we use credit to buy things we don't need, to impress people we don't like, and then we find ourselves stressed out trying to pay off our debts.

Please, don't tell me you're waiting for prince charming to come and help you solve your debt issues. You're planning to marry rich, or marry a magician who will make all your troubles disappear. Well I hate to have to be the one to tell you – there ain't no man that can solve your debt issues. The way things are going these days he will probably quadruple your debt by the time he adds his.

And Don't tell me debt is not a big deal. Debt will cut off your legs and laugh at you as you grovel in the dirt begging for mercy. If you don't need it, don't get it. If you can't afford it, don't get it. If you're already in debt, get out quickly. If you think you'll never get out, you're right, you won't.

32 THEIR THOUGHTS ARE NOT YOURS

"Most people are other people. Their thoughts are someone else's opinions, their lives a mimicry, their passions a quotation." – Oscar Wilde

"I wonder if they think my dress is too tight; I wonder if they are all wondering when I will get married; I wonder if he thinks I'm greedy since I have so much food on my plate; I wonder if everyone is still thinking about me tripping down the stairs."

We spend so much time worrying about what other people are thinking about us. The funny thing is that we are all so busy thinking about our own lives that we barely have time to think about and acknowledge the existence of other people around us. So when you find yourself wondering what people are thinking about you, realize that they are probably not even thinking about you at all.

Yes you may have made a mistake, and you feel like you will never live it down. Don't worry about it, most people have already forgotten about it, while the rest of them are so busy trying to fix their own lives that don't really care about your mistakes.

We all have **busy lives**, and fortunately (or unfortunately) for you, we are all a little self-absorbed, so if it doesn't concern us, we don't spend too much time thinking about it. When you find yourself wondering… "I wonder what he is thinking about me," or "I wonder what she is thinking about me"… forget it, they are most likely not even thinking about you at all.

Therefore, since we are surrounded by such a great cloud of witnesses, let us throw off everything that hinders and the sin that so easily entangles, and let us run with perseverance the race marked out for us.   — HEBREWS 12:1 NIV

31 SPEND TIME WITH KIDS

"All grown-ups were once children... but only few of them remember it."
– Antoine de Saint-Exupéry

Every time I'm around my niece, I learn something new. I learn that there are more important things to life, like laughing and smiling and squeezing yourself into a four-feet tall cardboard house, just so you can spend hours playing "knock knock."

Kids are the most amazing creatures in the world! They are so smart and so confident and so capable of doing the most awesome things. To them impossible is a stupid word. They are very trusting, yet very wise – and so full of curiosity. Sometimes when I take a walk with my niece I notice things that had always been there, but I was just too busy to notice. She looks at the grass and touches it and tries to taste it. She looks at the fire hydrant and asks me for the hundredth time to tell her what it's called, which I patiently and willingly do, no matter how many times she asks. She hears a dog barking in the distance and asks if it's a dog? Yes little one it's a dog. When things start to scare her, she holds my hands tightly, but other times she explores and she learns something new every time.

When we spend time with kids we realize how much of life we are missing, and how delicious life could really be if we let it. We learn that what we think is so important and so serious is not nearly as important or as serious as we think it is. We learn to be confident again, because if we are patient enough to continue encouraging kids, we must be patient to continue encouraging ourselves. We learn to trust again, because if this little one can trust us, even though we have made many mistakes, then we can trust others even though they may make many mistakes.

30 PICK INTIMATE FRIENDS WISELY

"Everyone wants to ride with you in the limo, but what you want is someone who will take the bus with you when the limo breaks down." – *Oprah Winfrey*

We all long to belong, to connect, to feel like we are accepted for who we are. When we meet people who seem to accept us in all our "mess," we get really eager. We want to turn them into best friends or sometimes we want to make them our spouses immediately. The problem with this is that it all takes time. It takes time to really get to know someone. It takes time to really know how you feel about someone. It takes time to feel like you can be comfortable with someone. It takes time to feel like you can truly trust someone. It takes time to know if this person is trustworthy and worthy of your time, because time is the only thing you can never get back.

Does this person value what you value? Or will you always have disagreements about values? If you value honesty and integrity, and your intimate friend doesn't, there will always be disappointments. If you value chastity and your intimate friend doesn't, there will be times when your inner voice and your friend's voice will be suggesting you do two completely different things.

Your intimate friend doesn't have to believe the exact same things you do, but they must have the same values you do, or else you will find yourself in some strange guy's house doing things you never dreamed of doing, and wondering how you let yourself get convinced into thinking this was a good idea.

29 SET GOALS

"Reach high, for stars lie hidden in your soul. Dream deep, for every dream precedes the goal." – Mother Teresa

There are many things we wish would happen. I often wish that I could have so much money that I would never have to worry about money again, or that I knew who my future husband would be (so that when those random guys came up to me I could just smile and say "no thanks"), or that carrot-cake-cupcake with almond sprinkles would not taste oh so delicious (or that if they continued tasting delicious then at least they would be zero calories). But wishing and setting goals are two completely different things.

When we decide to lose weight, or to stop a bad habit, or to spend more time with family, if we don't have a plan to accomplish what we have set out to do, then what we are doing is just wishing. When we are serious about accomplishing something, we must create a goal, and come up with a plan to help us accomplish that goal. The problem is not that you don't have any creative ideas, the problem is that you don't accomplish your goals, you don't complete your ideas. What are you waiting for? Are you waiting for someone else to implement your ideas? How would you feel if you saw your idea somewhere else months from now? Give yourself the permission to be phenomenal!

I know there are probably hundreds of things you would like to do, or change, or become, but we must start with one. Just one. There is incredible power in focus. So pick one thing you would like to do, and give yourself a month to accomplish this goal (or at least a major part of the goal), and then go ahead and be fabulously you.

28 GIVE

"To give pleasure to a single heart by a single act is better than a thousand heads bowing in prayer." – Mahatma Ghandi

The amazing thing about giving is that not only does it have an amazing way of coming back to you many times and in many more ways than you could have imagined, but the very act of giving and depriving yourself motivates you to think of ways to accomplish your goals despite what you no longer have.

The other day, I wanted to attend a conference, but I also really wanted to give to this charity. I had been procrastinating giving to the charity for months, until finally I decided that I would just give to them, and figure out how to pay for the conference some other way. The funny thing is that I was able to volunteer to help out with the conference and only had to pay half of what the conference was worth! I ended up getting my money back almost immediately because giving that money forced me to think of other more creative ways to accomplish my goals.

Whatever it is you are really desiring, give it away. If it's companionship, give it to someone else, and just listen to them and be there. If it's money, give it to someone who is less fortunate. If it's encouragement, give it to others. If it's friendship, become the best friend you can be to others. If it's time, serve others with your time. You will be amazed to see how much more of everything you have when you are willing to freely give.

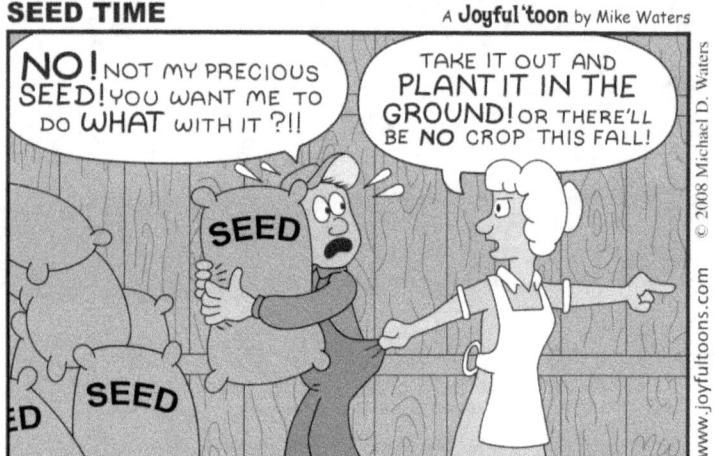

Now he who supplies seed to the sower and bread for food will also supply and increase your store of seed and will enlarge the harvest of your righteousness. 2 CORINTHIANS 9:10 NIV

27 LEARN TO QUIT

*"**Q is for Quitting:** Sticking things out is overrated, particularly if you stick out the wrong things. In fact, I think you'd be much better off quitting most of what you do so you have the resources to get through the hard slog I call the Dip... The challenge, then is to not quit in the Dip, but instead to quit everything else so you have the focus to get through the slog of what matters."* – Seth Godin

Growing up I was always told that winners never quit, and quitters never win, but sometimes we have to quit. We have to quit things (or people) that are bad for us, we have to **quit doing work** we are not passionate about, so we can spend more time pursuing our passion. There is a time and place for everything, including quitting.

When we do things we are not passionate about they deplete and drain us. Instead of feeling excited and invigorated at the end of the day, we feel exhausted and are glad when the day is over…what a horrible waste of life and talent! When we do things we are passionate about, we feel energized, we are in a place of "flow," time seems to fly by so beautifully and we don't get tired. We feel like we are living, breathing and being for the first time every time. We get to a place where our passion smiles at us, hugs us and says "welcome home, I've been waiting for you." But until we get to that place, we are only wasting time. So why not be a better steward of your life and time, and start strategically quitting now.

Quitting is not giving up, it's choosing to focus your attention on something more important. Quitting is not losing confidence, it's realizing that there are more valuable ways you can spend your time. Quitting is not making excuses, it's learning to be more productive, efficient and effective instead. Quitting is letting go of things (or people) that are sucking the life out of you so you can do more things that will bring you strength.

26 ALWAYS DO THE RIGHT THING

"The time is always right to do the right thing." – *Martin Luther King Jr.*

I don't always do the right thing, and writing this section has made me feel like a horrible hypocrite, but the truth remains that it's important to always do the right thing no matter how hard it is.

A buddy of mine recently confronted me about using the online library resources for a state I no longer lived in. Since libraries in America are funded by state taxes, he was right, I was stealing. Even though he joked about it, and even though I had really good reasons and excuses, I could not deny that he was right, so I had to stop.

In this life we will always have to choose between right and wrong. When the right choice is easy, the choice is easy, but when the wrong choice is easier, we must learn and train ourselves to still choose the right thing. Yes it may be hard, yes it may be painful, but the right choice is always worth it. The right choice always rewards us in many more ways than we could have ever dreamed.

Imagine what your life would be like if you didn't always have to look over your shoulder. If you didn't have to worry about "getting caught." If you didn't worry whether you would later remember the story you were telling. Doing the wrong thing torments us and makes us feel worthless and guilty in the most ridiculous ways.

Choosing to do the right thing builds us up inside, and makes us happier with who we have chosen to be. And trust me, doing the right thing looks fabulous on you!

25 LOSE SOME

"You have two choices with annoying actions and behaviors of others: Deal with it or forget about it. But fretting is not an option." – Alan Weiss

Life is not a battle. Yet we spend so much time fighting. We always have to be right about everything. One time I was arguing with this guy over his consistent lateness whenever we tried to hang out, and he argued that he was not late at least one time. Of course I had to respond that I was sure he had been late, but he was lucky that I was too late to realize how late he was...yes that was literally our conversation, we both kept trying to prove the other person was wrong until we realized how ridiculous we sounded.

It's amazing how passionate we get about our own perspective and our own "rightness." But sometimes it's more important for us to let go of being right and instead let peace reign. Would you rather be right or would you rather be happy? I must confess sometimes I feel like I would rather be right than be happy, but being happy is always a superior choice.

Lose some arguments, let the other person feel heard, no matter how right you may be (or you may think you are). When you let things go, the truth always finds its way to you.

24 CONSIDER THE LESS PRIVILEGED

"If you find that not many of the things you asked for have come, and not perhaps quite so many as sometimes, remember that this Christmas all over the world there are a terrible number of poor and starving people." – J.R.R. Tolkien

The other day I found myself reading an **article in Poize Magazine** about **Stephanie Okereke** and her struggles to help end **VVF (Vesico Vaginal Fistula)** in Nigeria. VVF often occurs when girls are forced into marriage at a very young age and have prolonged labor, or during the various forms of female genital mutilation. And yes the practice continues today.

Many of the girls (and women) suffering from this ailment are victims simply because they were born where they were born, and in the families they were born in. They were not promiscuous or careless. They were just born into a family that chose their own way over the lives of their children, and into a society that protected tradition at the expense of life. The only treatment for VVF is re-constructive surgery. VVF is not a condition I would wish on my worst enemy (to really understand what goes on, read the article), and yet people are suffering in silence and shame everyday because of this condition.

Yes we all have problems, but maybe, just maybe your problems could be much worse. If nothing else, at least you're alive and you have the opportunity to do better tomorrow.

23 GARBAGE IN, GARBAGE OUT

"But until a person can say deeply and honestly, 'I am what I am today because of the choices I made yesterday,' that person cannot say, 'I choose otherwise.'" – *Stephen Covey*

When I first started learning to use a computer in school, the instructor told us about the magical way the computer worked:

Garbage in = Garbage out

If you put in the wrong thing into the computer, you get the wrong results – or what some of my friends like to call "user error."

Our minds are a gazillion times more complex than regular computers, but the same premise remains, we have to be careful what we put into our systems.

There are times when I get really upset and all these curse words bubble up from inside. Keep in mind that I don't use curse words, I believe that only lazy people curse because they would rather not take the time and the energy to express themselves more clearly – but that is a discussion for another time. And sometimes the curse words that come to my mind are so creative and so unlike anything you may hear regularly, that when I sit down to think about it I realize I heard the curse words in a movie (sometimes many, many years ago).

The millions of things we have learned from watching TV or from movies are so subtle that we don't even realize how much we have been influenced by what we watch. I mean seriously, who told you that you have to close your eyes when you kiss, or that the only way to avoid panty lines is wearing a thong, or that it's normal to get sick every time flu season hits, or that it's okay to curse people out when you get angry? We learn from what we surround ourselves with, and we never forget what we take in.

Don't think you can watch all the romantic movies, soap operas, TV shows and read all the romantic books out there and not be affected. Ninety-nine percent (99%) of the romantic stuff out there is garbage…and what you put in always comes out…uglier.

22 STOP CUSSIN' YOURSELF

"Words are, of course, the most powerful drug used by mankind." –
Rudyard Kipling

Our tongues are powerful!

When I was younger, my older brother and I would get
into fist fights. Since he was bigger and stronger than I was, I
would have to result to using my words:

*"You're so stupid, you're the stupidest idiot in the world…stupid
idiot!"*

Which just meant that we would start fighting again, and the
cycle would continue…

The thing about calling people names and using profanity
is that we only do it because we are ignorant of how to
express ourselves better, or we are too lazy to attempt to
express ourselves better. When we get angry and call someone
a 4-letter curse word, we have not expressed to them why we
are angry, what they have done to make us angry, how we can
find a solution to the challenge, or how we can prevent the

situation from happening again. All we have done is temporarily ease our anger, but in the end the words we use affects us more than the people we use them on.

Most of the time, the person we are upset with will just ignore us and go on with their lives, while we continue fuming for days, and let the anger fester within us. The words we use come back to bite us in the butt.

This is why it's also very important what you say to and about yourself. If you keep telling yourself that you'll never succeed, then guess what? You never will. And you will only have yourself to blame for it. The words you use on your children, or on your family members are incredibly powerful and can make or break those relationships, but the words you use on yourself is the most disastrous of them all.

Side note: some people argue that using curse words is great in music or other artistic forms because it shocks the system. Those people would be wrong. Yes it shocks the system, but it expresses nothing. Why not shock the system by expressing yourself, which is **what art is really supposed to be about**.

Set a guard over my mouth, O LORD;
keep watch over the door of my lips.   – PSALM 141:3 NIV

21 IT'S SOMEONE ELSE'S PROBLEM

"It isn't that they can't see the solution. It is that they can't see the problem." – G.K. Chesterton

You can't have survived for so long without learning how to solve problems. While we hate having problems, there is a thrill we get when it seems as if the solution to our problems came out of nowhere – and just in time.

While it is often easier to help other people solve their problems, we often find it hard to solve ours because we are so busy with all the emotions involved that we forget to be rational. So give yourself 10 minutes to imagine that whatever your are facing (loneliness?) is someone else's problem. Imagine that one of your best friends comes to you complaining of how lonely and tired she is. She doesn't think she will ever meet the "right guy," and she doesn't think that the "right guy" would even be interested in her.

What would you say to her in that situation? Would you tell her how beautiful and smart she is, and how any guy would be absolutely fortunate to have her? Would you tell her that she doesn't need to worry about meeting the guy but she should trust God, because he loves her so much and has promised to provide her with good things?

Imagine your other friend comes to tell you about how the situation is impossible, and she will never be able to accomplish her goals. What would you say to her? Would you tell her that she is brilliant and that God has something awesome planned for her?

Whatever you would say, march yourself to a mirror right now and say it to yourself! Because you ought to treat yourself at least as well as you treat your friends. After all, Jesus said you were worth it all – and that's only because you really ARE worth it all!

20 STOP WAITING ON GOD

"We have been deceived into believing prayer is all about persuading God to release His power. We believe He can save, heal, and deliver but that He is waiting on us to shape up and earn it. The truth is, we don't deserve it, and we will never be good enough. Because of Jesus, all that God has is ours. That's good news. We no longer need to beg or plead; we need to exercise the authority He has given us and receive His blessings." – Andrew Wommack

It feels great to say that you are "waiting on God." You are waiting for him to do something. Whenever He gets ready, he will do it. You feel holy, and pious and spiritual and well…after all it's important to learn to be patient. Please I beg you, for the love of God, just STOP!

God has already done everything he will ever do. He has done his part. It is up to you to trust him and do what he tells you to do. No I'm not advocating for you to do whatever you want to do and hope for the best. What I'm saying is stop doing nothing, just because you think it's better for you to just wait on God to do something. Instead go out and **live the life God has called you** to live.

Have faith, and God will show you the amazing things which **he has ordained for you since the beginning of time**. Resist evil and accept good, **God has already commanded you to fight**, don't say "He's allowing this to teach me something." No! God allows WHAT YOU ALLOW.

There's a difference between waiting with patient expectation, and waiting because you never know what God will do. If you don't know how God thinks or what God wants to do in your life, read the Bible. When you know what God wants you to do, Go out there and do it and see God work his wonderful mission through you.

The whole time you thought you were waiting on God, but the whole time God was waiting on you.

19 SPEND TIME GETTING REFRESHED

"True silence is the rest of the mind; it is to the spirit what sleep is to the body, nourishment and refreshment." – William Penn

I find myself being so busy and so tired often. On a good day I can get maybe six hours of sleep, on other days, I wake up wondering when I will get the next chance to crawl into bed.

The other day I was learning about the animals in the Bible, and I learned about how eagles live a long time, but they are **able to stay youthful because they shed their feathers and grow new feathers**. I thought about how life is supposed to be like that. We spend so much time being busy that we don't realize that **our lives are falling apart**. We think it's normal to be busy, to be sleep-deprived, to be exhausted, but God never wanted us to live this life like that. We have well-meaning friends and mentors who tell us "welcome to the new normal," "get used to being tired." But is that what God wants for us? God wants only good things for us!

God has promised us that he **will satisfy our desires so that we can be renewed like an eagle**. (That excites me!)

Whatever it is that refreshes you: Spending time with God, reading a good book, taking long walks, talking to friends, whatever it is – just do it.

When you feel tired, feel discouraged, feel like you want to give up, and there is no hope, remember to spend time getting refreshed. Remember that hope cannot be based on situations, but it must be based on who God is. Focus on God, refresh your soul, live fabulously.

18 IMAGINE SUCCESS

"If you are not happy, optimistic, and energetic when you first arise in the morning, you need to change some things about your life." – Alan Weiss

What does success look like to you? Does it mean a bigger house a shinier car, a lot more clothes? What exactly does it look like for you to be successful?

What would you do differently if you had all you wish you had?

Where would you go? What would you spend more time (or less time) doing? What charity would you give more money to, or spend more time serving? Who would you spend more time (or less time) with?

How would you live your life differently? How would you cherish your life more? What kind of story would you want your life to tell? Which kind of people would you like to be around? What kind of influence would you like to leave behind?

Whatever it is that you would do, start doing it now – and you will be surprised how acting successful usually leads to paths of success.

Imagine what a **successful life** would look like. Imagine what a successful career would look like. **Imagine how you would live if you never had to worry about failing**…and go out and live! The beautiful thing about trying is that you never fail, you may learn many ways that things won't work, but your experience will never be a waste! Failures are people who never try! The ball's in your court!

17 RECONNECT WITH OLD FRIENDS

"Friendship is certainly the finest balm for the pangs of disappointed love." – *Jane Austen*

The other day I went to the movie theatre to watch Midnight in Paris with a group of people, but only two of us showed up. This guy (let's call him G) and I. Everything went pretty well. He paid for the movies, I paid for the snacks, we found a nice quiet spot in the theatre and sat down to enjoy the movie. Surprisingly, the movie was really good, and I thoroughly enjoyed myself. There were some hilarious scenes and hilarious lines. Like this line by one of the main characters, Inez, after she thought the help had stolen her jewelry and her fiancé, Gil, tried to comfort her. Inez said "You always take the side of the help. That's why Daddy says you're a communist."

The whole movie was full of stupid lines like that and I found myself laughing (maybe guffawing might be a more appropriate word) wholeheartedly...that is until G leaned over and asked me "are you always this loud?" ouch! So for the entire night I was so self-conscious. I still enjoyed the movie, but I was not able to fully immerse myself into it…

A few days later, I was talking to one of my friends from high school (let's call her J). We talked about the most random things. I told her everything that was going on in my life, giving her all the highlights of my "blonde" moments, and she laughed with me. She never said I was too loud or too "blonde" or too anything. She just accepted me for me. And it reminded me of why I love her so much. You see to her, I'm never "loud" I'm just me, and to her being me is just right!

You need people like that in your life, if you don't have them, why not? And how soon can you change that?

16 MAKE NEW FRIENDS

"Friendship is born at that moment when one person says to another: "What! You too? I thought I was the only one." – *C.S. Lewis*

I made a new friend (at work) the other day. I just happened to run into her and I asked her what her name was. The next day I casually asked her what she was interested in, and we struck up a conversation. I even ended up introducing her to another friend who was currently working in the field she was interested in.

Now every time I see my new friend she smiles and talks a little. She used to keep to herself and look sad most of the day, but now she smiles. How exciting! I'm excited for her because she's probably glad to finally be able to talk to someone at work. But I'm also excited for me because I'm learning about the complexity of people and their lives. It's easy to make fun of the guy that stares at you at work, until you realize that he has complicated family issues that he has to deal with every night when he gets home (and sometimes during lunch breaks).

Investing in people is ALWAYS worth it! And it always yields a one-hundred percent (100%) return. Helping people reminds us that it's not all about us, and takes us out of our self-centered cocoon where the sky always seems to be falling.

Making friends is not just about helping you to no longer be lonely, but it's about thinking of ways to help others live better, richer lives. If someone's life is not enriched by their time with you, then you're not doing something right.

15 MAKE TIME FOR PEOPLE

"I've learned that every day you should reach out and touch someone. People love a warm hug, or just a friendly pat on the back." – Maya Angelou

People are time-consuming, but outside of spending time with God, there is no better way to spend your time. There are times when we are busy, and there are times when we are just pretending to be busy, and there are times when we would rather do anything (and I mean anything) than be around certain people, nevertheless, it's worth it to make time for people.

One Sunday, not that long ago church had ended and I was in a rush. I'm not really sure where I was in a rush to, or whether I was just pretending to be in a rush so I didn't have to look like I had nothing going on in my life (a discussion for another time). But there I was, rushing out of Church and two of the brightest most beautiful girls accosted me and started talking about their lives. It was the most beautiful thing ever. I don't quite remember what we said but I know that was probably one of the most interesting conversations I have had at that particular Church. We talked about school, about books, about where we saw ourselves in the future. I smiled so much, I wanted them to have a better life, and better opportunities. At the end of the conversation, they felt like they had been heard, and I felt like I was at the right place at the right time doing what God wanted me to do.

I could have just said "hi" and walked away, but listening to the girls not only made them feel good, it made me feel good as well. And that is the beautiful thing about giving, the giver always receives a much greater gift. So take the time to listen to people, it may be the first time in a long time that they actually experience that kind of quiet acceptance and acknowledgment.

14 LEARN TO "LIGHT UP"

"It takes courage to love, but pain through love is the purifying fire which those who love generously know. We all know people who are so much afraid of pain that they shut themselves up like clams in a shell and, giving out nothing, receive nothing and therefore shrink until life is a mere living death." – Eleanor Roosevelt

A few years ago, one of the ladies at my church pulled me aside and asked me whether I was interested in one of the guys at the church. She told me she noticed that I lit up whenever he was around. She was right. I did light up whenever he was around. I enjoyed talking to him and listening to his wisdom. But she missed something. I light up whenever anyone is around.

One of the greatest things I ever learned was that people really want to feel important. We all want to be missed when we are gone, and we all want to be wanted when we are around. It's easy for people to feel comfortable with you if you show them how excited you are to be around them. So I purposely try to light up whenever I'm talking to someone. Don't get me wrong, there are times when I don't "light up" around people as I should, and there are some people that are easier for me to "light up" around than others, but that doesn't change the fact that people are special and should be treated "special." We are all walking around with so much hurt and pain, we're just looking for people to accept us.

So how do you light up?

1. Always have a big smile when you see them
2. Think of how you would react if you were delighted by something (how expressive your face and hands and voice would be) and do that whenever you see them.
3. Remember something from your last conversation with them and follow up with them.
4. Remember their names and say it when you see them (whether they are old friends or new acquaintances)

Remember to let your light shine – it's the only light that some will ever see!

Side note: "Lighting up" is not "being fake." People can smell fake easily and we all get disgusted by fake people and fake compliments. "Lighting up" is just another way for saying that we should always remember to esteem the people around us, and let them know that we appreciate them, because they are much more valuable than we can comprehend. Don't believe me? Ask God.

13 PLEASE REMEMBER MY NAME

"Remember that a man's name is to him the sweetest and most important sound in the English language." - Dale Carnegie

"Wow that's a beautiful name! Can I call you 'O?'"
"No please call me Osayi."

Is there anything more annoying than someone telling you that they can't pronounce your name, so they would rather call you something else? Why don't they just take out your birth certificate, run it through the shredder and get one of those cattle-branding irons and brand you with this new name that they have graciously bestowed upon you.

Now imagine you're on the other side, and you think a person's name is too complicated, what do you do?

If it's not easy for you to pronounce, ask them to teach you. It doesn't matter how challenging a person's name is, don't try to make up a nickname for them. If they can take the effort to learn and remember your name, you should take the effort to learn and remember their name.

When you remember a person's name, you're telling them that you value them, and that time spent between the two of you, no matter how infrequent, is valuable to you. And you know we all just want to be valued. I can't tell you how many times I have surprised people by remembering their names. It doesn't take a whole lot of effort, but it's worth it. Strangers become best friends, enemies become comrades. Try it for yourself.

So you want a shortcut to making new friends instantly? Remember our names! It means the world to us.

12 BE PATIENT WITH LIFE

"I do know that waiting on God requires the willingness to bear uncertainty, to carry within oneself the unanswered question, lifting the heart to God about it whenever it intrudes upon one's thoughts. It's easy to talk oneself into a decision that has no permanence – easier sometimes than to wait patiently." – Elisabeth Elliot (Passion and Purity: Learning to Bring Your Love Life Under Christ's Control)

I've read so many books about finding your passion, and fulfilling your purpose. Sometimes the books meant to inspire you actually bring you down because you feel like you're not doing much with what God has given you. You feel a little disappointed because you're not quite where you expected yourself to be at this time, or you're not where you think God wants you to be. It can all be so discouraging. The important thing to remember though is that life is a journey. If we all arrived at our destination as soon as we made a decision, there wouldn't be a story to tell, and life wouldn't be very interesting.

We all have plans and goals, we all have places we would like to be by certain times. I remember my roommate from

College would always say how she wanted to start having kids by twenty-four (24), and she wanted to be married by twenty-three (23). She was 22 single and with no reasonable prospect in sight. I understood where she was coming from, but she was giving herself unnecessary pressure. Who says that if you don't have kids before thirty (30) you will not be able to have fun with them. Who says if you don't make your incremental million at a young age you will not be successful in life.

Yes incremental success is always great, and that is the way it happens many times, but sometimes we may feel like we are beating our heads against the wall and going nowhere and then something happens and we have exponential success!

Don't be discouraged by where you are. Life is not linear and cannot be easily charted with a mathematical equation... Life is organic!

Cast all your anxiety on him because he cares for you.
– 1 PETER 5:7 NIV

11 EMBRACE IMPERFECTION

"Better to do something imperfectly than to do nothing flawlessly." Robert Schuller

I bet you can list five things right now that you don't like about yourself. Maybe it's your hair and how it's not as straight or as curly as you wished it was, or your eyes are not as pretty as your friend's, or no matter how hard you work out you can't seem to get rid of that gut that protrudes in the most unflattering manner. You were upset because all your friends hit puberty before you, but when you finally got there you were upset that it hit you worse than them. Not only do you have to deal with a very painful monthly visitor, but you are endowed with assets that no matter how hard you try to cover them, men can't help but be distracted around you. You think your nose would have been better straighter, or that you would look better with dimples, or if only you didn't have those freckles, or those skinny legs, or your less than coke bottle figure, your whole life would be perfect. Well guess what?:

Imperfection is here to stay, so I guess you better get used to it.

Stop killing yourself trying to be a perfectionist. Nothing in this life is perfect, nothing can be perfect, we were all created to be good, but not perfect. The quest for perfection is a road filled with turmoil and disappointment.

Why exactly are we so bothered by imperfection. We think we will not be attractive unless we are perfect, or that we will not be able to get what we want unless we are perfect. But life often proves us wrong. When despite our imperfections other people still manage to find us attractive, and we still manage to be successful in getting what we want, do we correct our theories, no we just go on believing what we want. We actually think that making decisions from these beliefs created by our younger, less experienced selves is wise.

True beauty lies in contentment with imperfection- it's your prerogative to choose whether you believe it or not, either way, it's true.

10 YOU NEVER STOP THINKING

"The world as we have created it is a process of our thinking. It cannot be changed without changing our thinking" – Albert Einstein

The other day I was listening to **a podcast about Lays potato chips**. Keep in mind that I stopped snacking a few months ago when I learned how snacking messes with our digestive process. But there I was listening to this podcast at 8:24 am, and what did I do? I went to the vending machine, bought a bag of Lays potato chips, and ate it all up before you could say **supercalifragilisticexpialidocious**. Don't tell me you are not affected by what you hear. Don't tell me you are not affected by what you think and focus on.

Like breathing, we often forget that we are always thinking. When we are happy we are thinking happy thoughts, when we are sad, we are thinking sad thoughts, when we are angry – you got it, we're thinking angry thoughts. So when you feel yourself getting sad, make a conscious effort to think about happier thoughts from the past, or anticipate happy events in the future.

Our thinking is tied to our thoughts, you can't feel horrible without actually thinking horrible thoughts, whether that is rehashing something that happened in the past, or something bad we think will happen to us in the future. Sometimes we just have to let things go, whether or not they are working out the way we expected. We have to take control of our thoughts and decide what we will and will not do, and what we can and cannot do.

Don't let bad thoughts deceive you into thinking that you have to feel bad. Be aware and conscious of it, and choose to think good thoughts whenever you are bombarded with the bad.

Remember to live your life passionately!

Fix these words of mine in your hearts and minds; tie them as symbols on your hands and bind them on your foreheads.
— DEUTERONOMY 11:18 NIV

9 YOUR FUTURE IS SO BRIGHT

"I've decided that if there are only going to be a handful of Christians who really encounter God, who actually experience the abundant 'promised land life' He has come to give, then I want to be one of those few. You too?" – *Priscilla Shirer (One in a Million)*

A year or so ago I found some of my old journals from high school. In my journals I talked about my "crushes" and how I "super-duper" crushed on this guy, but I was only "minorly crushing" on this other guy. It was so cute and so funny. One entry that really stood out to me was the one about college. I was wailing about how life is not fair, and how I wouldn't be able to go to college because my parents would not be able to afford it, and I was sure I wouldn't get any scholarships. The sky was falling, and my life was definitely OVER!

Looking back now many years later, I did go to college, I got some scholarships and my parents paid for the rest, and I also went to law school on a full scholarship, I want to turn back time and tell myself "girl stop worrying, your future is so bright!"

"One day you will be a fancy writer/blogger/[insert whatever]/cool person so don't worry about it."

Whenever I face challenges today I try to remember those times and how I felt like even God could not fix that situation. But of course I was wrong. So if I was wrong then, I'm sure I will be wrong again…it may seem impossible, but with God Impossible is STUPID!

So what do you want to be? A doctor, or a writer, or a geologist, or something no one has even heard of before? Just go ahead and begin, imagine what you would do if you knew you could never fail, then begin doing it, because guess what? You can't fail.

Remember your future is so bright I have to squint to look at it!

Fight the good fight of the faith.   – 1 TIMOTHY 6:12 NIV

8 FREELY MAKE MISTAKES

"5 kinds of people who fail: The undecided. The unfocused. The untaught. The unexcited. The unthankful." – Dr. Mike Murdock

I did say earlier that you can't fail, but I guess I should clarify that there are times when you can, and you will fail. You fail when you do nothing. You fail when you are too afraid to try something. You fail when you let everyone else dictate who you are supposed to be. You fail when you choose not to become who you were created to be because it seems too hard, or too scary or too uncomfortable.

I used to hate driving to places I had never been before. Even when **Mr. Tom-Tom** (My GPS) was directing me and telling me how to get where I wanted to go safely, I would still get so tense and worry about getting lost or my car getting stuck in some village far away from civilization without a way of escape, just because I turned left, instead of right (I know I know, dramatic much?).

But one day I was coming back home after picking up a nightstand I had bought online and the worst thing happened!

I got lost. I made the wrong turn, and ignored Mr. Tom-Tom multiple times and didn't get back to my house until forty-five (45) minutes later. I was tired and I had wasted $13 worth of gas. But you know what happened, I realized that it didn't kill me! This whole time I was worried about getting lost, but the experience of getting lost was not as bad as I imagined it to be...and even better I learned that this particular road was not the one to take next time.

"Just because something doesn't do what you planned it to do doesn't mean it's useless." – *Thomas Edison*

So the next time you are tempted to be afraid of making a mistake. Purposely make the mistake, and you will realize there was nothing to be feared, but much to be gained!

7 MAKE PEOPLE FEEL NEEDED

"Always go to other people's funerals, otherwise they won't come to yours." – Yogi Berra

High school was one of the "funnest" yet most challenging times of my life. There was a lot of backbiting, fighting, hating and betrayal, which sometimes threatened to overtake all the good times. So as a coping mechanism I learned to treat people as if they were dispensable. I would act as if I didn't need them. When they hurt me or left my life I would say "well good riddance! I don't need them anyway." The problem with this attitude is that it was self-fulfilling. By acting like I didn't need people they decided that it was in their best interest to go where they were needed instead. Although I was hurting inside, I pretended as if I didn't care.

We all want to be needed. We all long to belong. So when we act as if we don't need people, there is no reason for them to stay. No I'm not saying that you should go crying to everybody you meet asking them to be your source of hope, but let people know that you are truly glad you met them, and that your life is enriched with them in it. Yes we shouldn't always make decisions based on feelings, and yes people (like me) who stay away from people who ignore them are probably not "confident and secure in themselves," but who likes to be around people who always ignore them? Who likes to be around people who won't even notice when they're gone?

6 OPINIONS ARE LIKE NOSES

"Opinions are like noses. We all have one and we all have holes in them." – Andrew Wommack

I once dated an amazing guy. Things didn't work out, and we broke up. One of my roommates at the time reminded me of how amazing he was, and how she could tell that he cared about me because he always held my hand when we crossed the street, and he always tried to make sure I was protected from those crazy and reckless Philadelphia drivers. I spent many months wondering if we had made a mistake ending the relationship, and if that would be my only opportunity for happiness. What I later realized was that just because he was amazing did not necessarily mean that I needed to spend the rest of my life with him.

Sometimes when I tell my stories, people look at me in disbelief. "What if that was the love of your life?" some of them would always ask. The love of my life? Seriously? If he was THE love of my life then he would be IN my life.

As women we often get so caught up in some other person's definition of what life is supposed to be. We're all supposed to meet our prince charming while we're singing in the forest. And when he meets us, he is irresistibly attracted to our beautiful voices and sunny blonde hair and we get married the next day and live happily ever after. Disney's idea of love is not true. It's great to watch the movies and feel the warm feelings, but in the end, we have to figure out what is true. Your friend's opinion of what your life should look like is not always true. Your parents' opinion of who you should be is not always true.

Everyone has opinions. Your parents think they know what's best for you, your friends think they know you better than you know yourself, marketers think they can motivate you to do whatever they want you to do, since they know you so well. And for some reason, you believe them.

So what if you're too short to be average height, or your hair is too kinky to be straight, or your nose is too broad to be pointy or your teeth are too jagged to be perfect? When people reject something about you, shrug it off, everyone is entitled to their own opinion. The same advice they give you is the same advice they would never take if they were you. The same thing that they say is ugly about you is the same thing that makes you uniquely and fabulously you. We don't need any more of those people, we don't need you to be like everyone else, we need you.

5 GOD DOES NOT ORDAIN LONELINESS

"Often a Christian man or woman falls prey to that cruel and vexatious spirit, wondering how to find marriage, who, when, where? It is on God that we should wait, as a waiter waits--not for but on the customer--alert, watchful, attentive, with no agenda of his own, ready to do whatever is wanted. 'My soul, wait thou only upon God; for my expectation is from him.' (Ps. 62:5 KJV) In Him alone lie our security, our confidence, our trust. A spirit of restlessness and resistance can never wait, but one who believes he is loved with an everlasting love, and knows that underneath are the everlasting arms, will find strength and peace." –
Elisabeth Elliot (Quest for Love: True Stories of Passion and Purity)

There are so many scriptures in the Bible where God calls us to separate ourselves for Him. To take some time out just spending time with Him. He wants us to be alone with Him, so we can quietly learn what He wants to teach us. I remember when I first started learning about the **love and grace of God**. I couldn't sleep much at night, I spent so many hours reading the Bible and listening to **Andrew Wommack's** CD's about the **goodness of God**. It had started out being one of the hardest years of my life (break ups and major life decisions), but it ended up being a year of tremendous growth.

The dictionary defines the difference between lonely and being alone:

> _Lonely:_ _affected with, characterized by, or causing a depressing feeling of being alone; lonesome._

> _Alone:_ _separate, apart, or isolated from others._

It's hard to fight the depression if you think God is the one oppressing you with loneliness.

Yes, God wants us to take time out from our busy schedules, to separate ourselves from others and spend time with Him. But, he never wants us feeling depressed about being alone in his presence — Don't be fooled by the devil. Fight him! Resist Him! And watch him run away like the snot-blowing coward he is.

4 DON'T YOU MISS ME?
(AND OTHER GUILT TRIPS)

"Pack your bags, we're going on a guilt trip!" – Jimmy Buffett

When I was growing up, I had family members that were travel agents for all expense paid guilt trips. Whenever you talked to them they would whine about how you never talked to them anymore and how they were disappointed to realize that you would treat them like that. It was pretty depressing to listen to them. It almost made me forget that communication was a two-way street.

Every now and then I get a phone call or a text message saying how bad it is that I don't *miss* somebody or call them or something of that nature. I usually respond with "I'm fine. How are you?"

When a person tries to make you feel guilty for not calling them or talking to them more often, that is an unhealthy relationship. When a person gets upset that you don't feel guilty when they want you to, that is an immature person.

Being around people like that will wear you out and make you feel awful. You can never make them happy, because you can never talk to them enough. If you don't call them, they get upset that you haven't called them, and when you do call them, they ask if you only remembered them because you are making your rounds today. And if you actually send them a text message telling them that you hope they have a good day, they will ask if you just forwarded that text message to everyone in your address book. Stay away from them. No seriously these people are leeches, STAY AWAY from them, you deserve better. You deserve to be fabulously sane.

3 THE FEMINIST LIE

"Nowadays, women grow up thinking that the essence of womanhood is the exercise of personal power (including sexual power). They've been taught to be loud, brash, sexual, aggressive, independent, and demanding....And because feminist ideas about womanhood stand in direct opposition to who God created woman and man to be, it has become increasingly difficult to make relationships work." – Mary Kassian (The Church in a post-feminist world)

When I was in undergrad I took a class on Women's studies. **I learned that men were the source of all my problems**. I learned that men created painful stilettos and then told me I had to wear them to get their attention. I learned that men took all the high-paying jobs and then left me to suffer with the low-paying-demoralizing jobs.

Then I went home and watched TV shows that showed me that not only were men nasty bullies but they were also **so stupid that they needed their witty and vivacious wives (or mothers)** to save their butts before the end of each episode.

Then I would listen to the songs on the radio that told me how I needed to be an independent woman who could take care of herself and had absolutely no need for a man, and therefore would be foolish to desire a man (even though these musicians frequently "sacrificed" independent-womanhood for marriage). Because after all, every man out there was a **two-timing-no-good-pervert who** was just waiting to be caught.

Then I would watch movies about how women who were wise and mature were more open with their **sexuality** and would sleep with whomever (or whatever) they were attracted to, whenever they felt the urge. And how those who were sexual prudes were just **immature ignorant little girls** who needed to be laughed at and mocked, and maybe even disabused of their ignorant notions. So being the **not-easily-influenced** adult that I was, I gladly accepted the feminist lie.

The truth is women need men, we are neither superior nor inferior to men. We are better at some things and worse at some things. Mature people take the hard road and choose to delay quick gratification for true love. Mature people realize that the world does not revolve around them, and their desires, but around commitment. Mature people are committed to something beyond themselves; God, good, the good of society, family etc. If men are the source of your problems then you are doomed to wait for eternity for them to fix it.

Don't be ignorant (or maybe stupid?) like I was, when I believed **the feminist lie**, read the **Bible** and learn about true womanhood.

2 GET MORE STUFF

"If you're so shallow that you think stuff will make you happy, when you get some stuff you'll find out that you're shallow" – *Dave Ramsey*

We all know that getting more stuff makes us happier right? Stuff can make us look hotter, live longer, be more attractive, more popular, more admired, more interesting, more everything…

Dave Ramsey's quote about getting more stuff is one of my favorites because I get so caught up thinking about how my life would be so much better if I had more money, if I could just get this bill paid, or if I could just get this thing that I've been wanting for so long; if only I could get that new car, or that new house, or that new computer, then I could finally be happy!

The bad news is that getting more stuff does not make us happy. The good news is that we can choose to be happy whether or not we have all the stuff we always wanted. Life is so funny – we can choose to be satisfied with what we have, or we can live a life of dissatisfaction regardless of what we have.

How many times have you looked forward to buying an item with anticipation, thinking that once you got that item, all would be right with the world, your life would be complete and as soon as you got the item, you started thinking about the next thing you had to get to once again "complete" your life, while the item sat in the corner gathering dust and cobwebs.

We spend a lot of time trying to get more and more things not realizing that those things can never fulfill us. Learn from those who have gone before you – stuff can never satisfy your desires, so focus on **the ONE** who can.

1 KICK! BITE! SCREAM! FIGHT: BULLY THE BULLIES!

"Never, never, never give in!" – Winston Churchill

My first year of high school was tough. I was always getting bullied. The kids teased me about my African accent, they teased me about my forehead, they teased me about my full lips, they teased me about my skinny legs. Pretty much anything that was beautiful and unique about me they teased me about. There was one particular student who picked me as his favorite person to bully. He was really tall, husky, a little slow and very intimidating. He sat behind me in Mr. Garcia's Geography class and we had one empty seat between us. Every day on my way to my seat he would stick his foot out to trip me. Then when I finally got to my seat he would push the empty chair into mine and would give me crazy headaches for the rest of the day. I tried to play nice and just ignore him. Then I tried to be nice to him to pacify him, then I tried to stay out of his way, but it was impossible, and I had to deal with him in that class every single day.

One day I on my way to pick up an assignment from Mr. Garcia's desk I heard him snickering. And on the way back, I found out why. This big bully tried to trip me – not realizing that this was not the day to mess with me. I dropped my assignment and pushed him as hard as I could. I pushed with both my hands on his chest as forcefully as I could. I just kept pushing and screaming at him, yelling about how he needed to leave me alone and stop bothering me, and how I wasn't afraid of him. I kept pushing and pushing until Mr. Garcia separated us. Everyone looked at me like "oh no! the African kid snapped" but I didn't care. After that day Geography class was the most peaceful class ever. Sometimes the bully would still try to bug me, but he realized that I wouldn't be pushed around anymore.

Depression and Loneliness are twin bullies. They come into your life when you least expect it. Make a home in your house and verbally abuse you. They tell you that you are worth nothing, that you will never be happy and that God will never give you what you desire. Depression and Loneliness are liars and they can never be trusted. Whenever you hear them speaking, I give you permission to get angry! Don't try to pacify them, don't try to talk rationally to them, don't try to appease them. The only way to deal with them is to fight like your life depended on it – because it does.

When you hear Depression and Loneliness talking, I give you permission to kick, bite scream and fight in your own special way and you know what? They'll think twice about coming back.

Remember life is meant to be won!

And having disarmed the powers and authorities, he made a public spectacle of them, triumphing over them by the cross.
— COLOSSIANS 2:15 NIV

O* (Bonus) Focus on God's Love

Sometimes my niece and I don't see eye to eye, maybe it's because she's only two years old, and she's trying to figure out her independence, but whatever the case, those times can be very challenging because it means somebody is about to get hurt, and it probably won't be me.

When I ask my niece to stand still while we're in the parking lot as I quickly get something out of the car, and she moves, it's because she doesn't understand. When I tell my niece that she can't have any more yogurt, because she has eaten nothing but yogurt all day and that eating different flavors of yogurt does not constitute a balanced diet, and she gets upset, it's because she doesn't understand. When I ask my niece to go to bed because we'll have to wake up early in the morning the next day, and she begins to cry, it's because she doesn't understand. It feels to her like I am depriving her of something good, but she doesn't understand that I'm only trying to give her something much, much better.

Sometimes I forget how much God loves me. When he tells me not to tell lies, but I do because it's easier to tell a lie at the time than to tell the truth, it's because I don't understand. When I choose to steal because I have a bill to pay, when God has already promised to provide all my needs, it's because I don't understand. When I lay in bed sick all day, when God told me I didn't have to be sick since he already took all my pain and diseases on the cross, it is because I don't understand. And When God tells me he forgives me for everything, and I still feel guilty and stay away from him, it's because I don't understand.

Let's learn about God's love together. Everything he says and does is because he wants the best for us. If he didn't love us, then there would be no point to his words, but because he does, we can truly say that there is nothing impossible with him. We can truly say that **Impossible is Stupid**. So let's focus on God's love, because it's all that matters.

I thought it was appropriate to end this book by encouraging you to focus on God's love in everything. This does not mean that you live a careless and selfish life, but that you live everyday realizing that you were created on purpose and for a purpose and since God is on your side, you have no excuse for not succeeding.

Although many of the truths I shared in this book are applicable whether or not you believe in Jesus, all of that doesn't matter in the end because you need Jesus to show you who you were truly meant to be, and how much you are truly loved.

If you don't have a relationship with Jesus Christ then today is a very exciting day for you because you can finally start living your fabulous life now. It's not hard, you don't have to earn it, you don't have to wait until you have it all figured out or you stop doing all the things that make you feel guilty. All you have to do is truly believe that Jesus is the only way, the only one that can make you whole and then say it out loud so that your whole being can hear it (Romans 10:11).

Please send me an email (info@iyasostuff.com) and I will send you a free **WELCOME TO THE FAMILY** *packet.*

~~THE END~~

The Beginning...

For **with God** nothing shall be impossible.
(Luke 1:37, KJV)

ABOUT THE AUTHOR

 Osayi Osar-Emokpae is the only daughter of Dr. & Mrs. Osar-Emokpae. She lives to glorify God and bring honor to her family in everything she does.

She is gifted to encourage, and that's why she writes.

You can find out more about her work at:

Iyasostuff.com/programs

Her other writings include:
Chosen: 366 daily devotionals for young folks (Coming Soon)
Late Twenties Woman (Poem Series)
There is no "there" there

Don't miss your FREE goodies
(FREE audio guide download, FREE action guide, *and more*)
for this book at:

Impossible.Iyasostuff.com